TODDLER COLORING BOOK

Copyright (c) Terrific Tot Coloring

square

circle

rectangle

triangle

semicircle

oval

apple

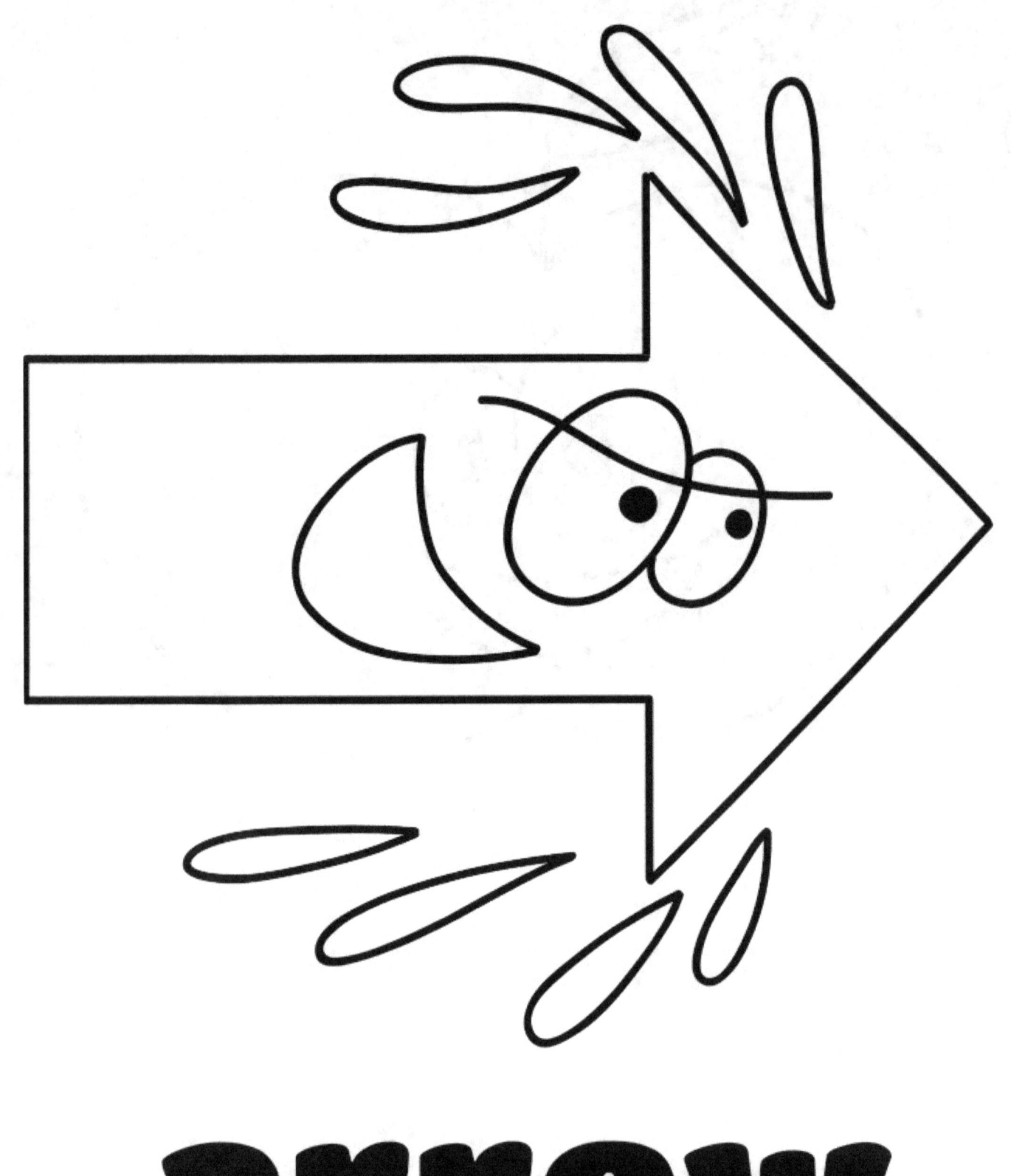

arrow

star

cloud

clover

moon
(crescent)

cross

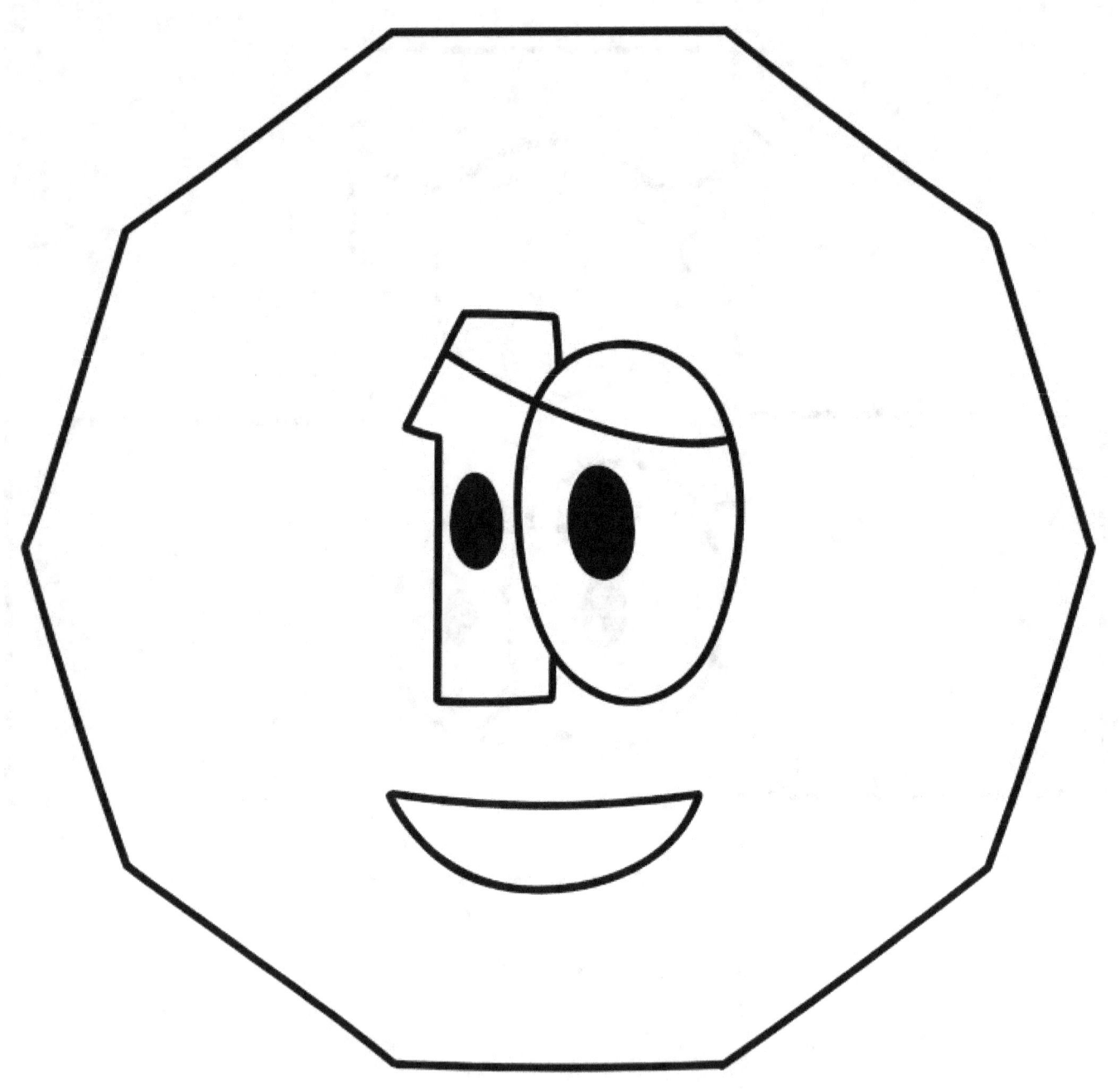

decagon

diamond

drop

ellipse

emerald

hand

heart

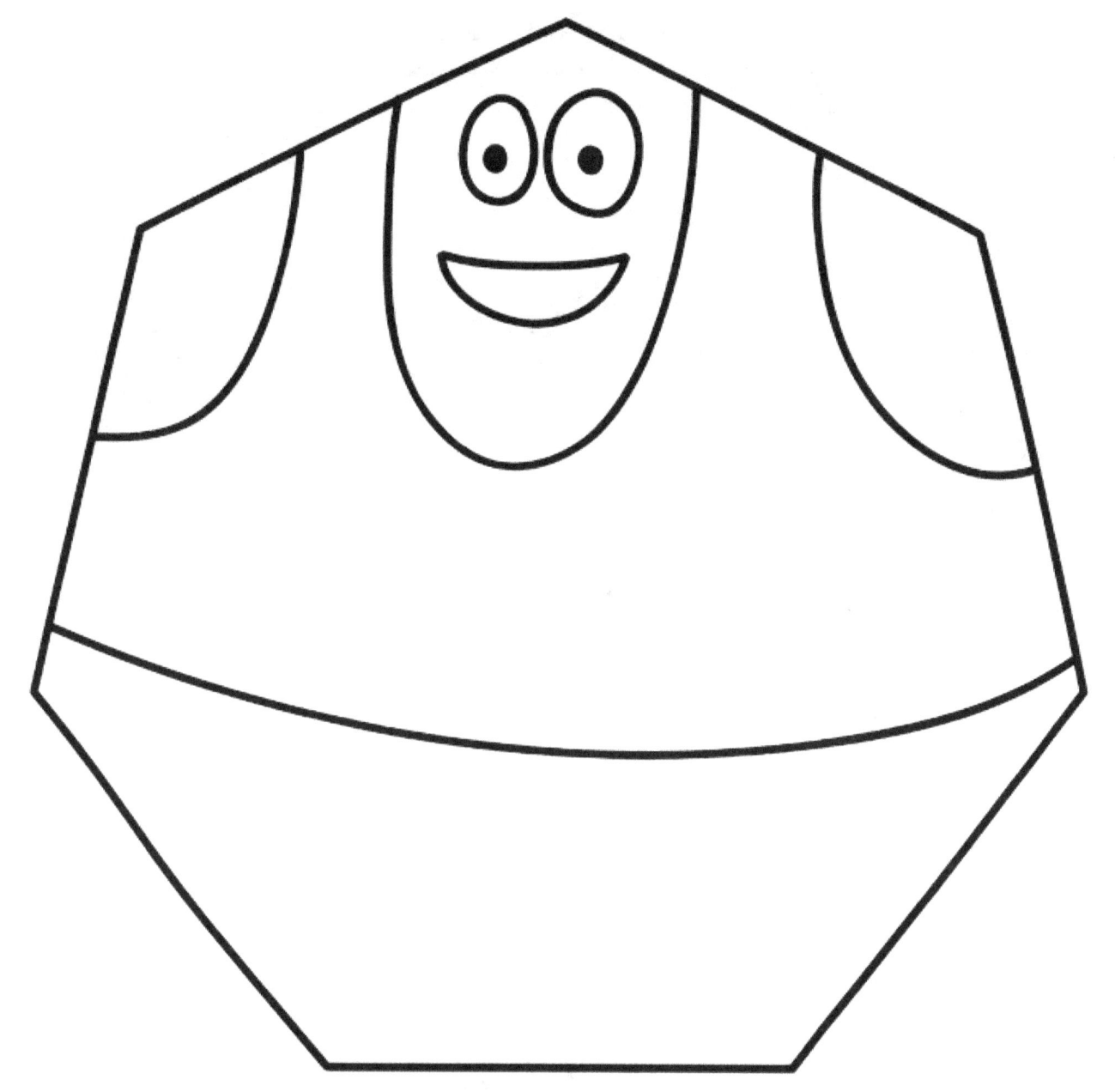

heptagon

hexagon

kite

marquise

nonagon

octagon

pentagon

pie

quadrant

rhombus

right triangle

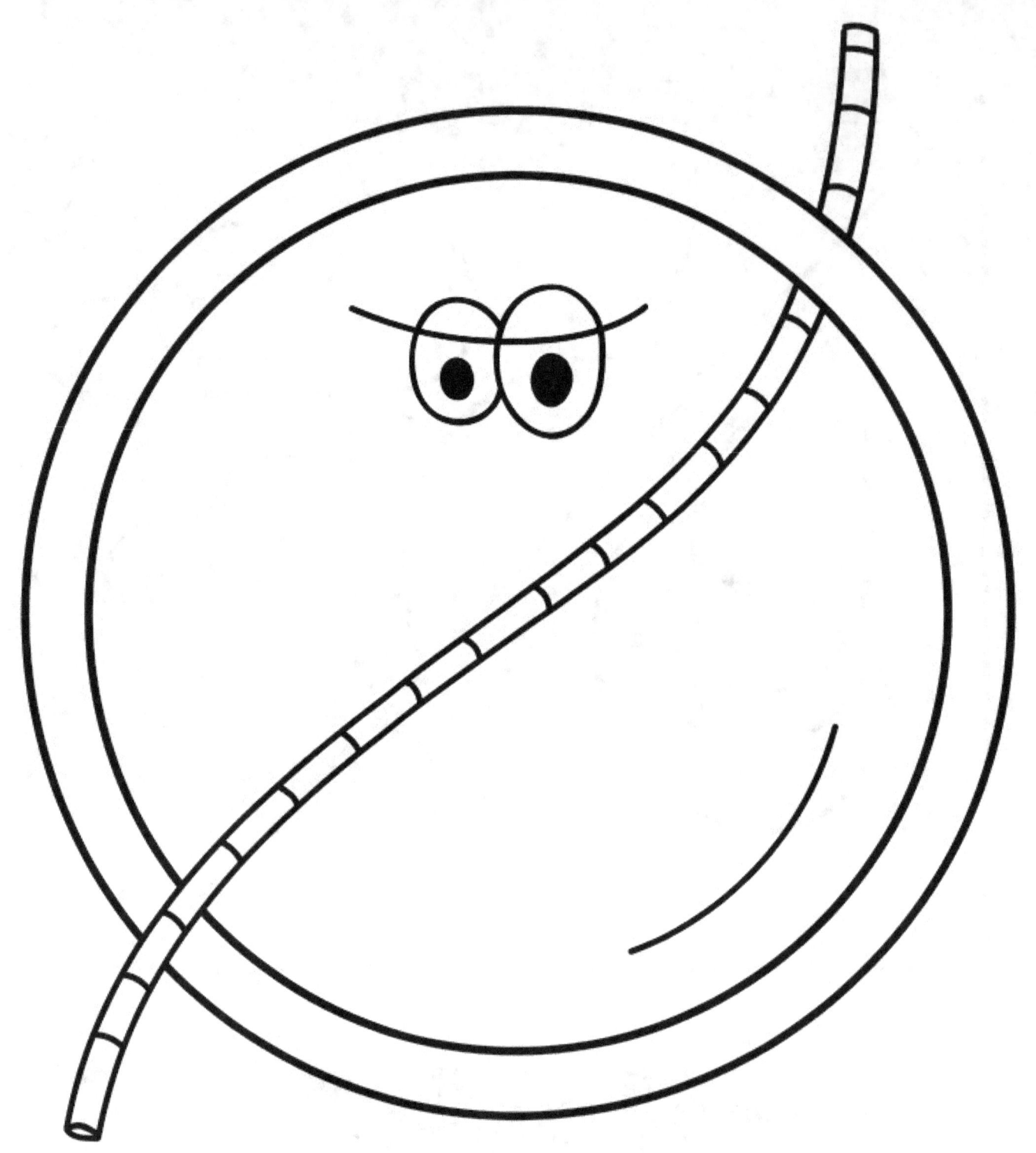

ring

trapezium

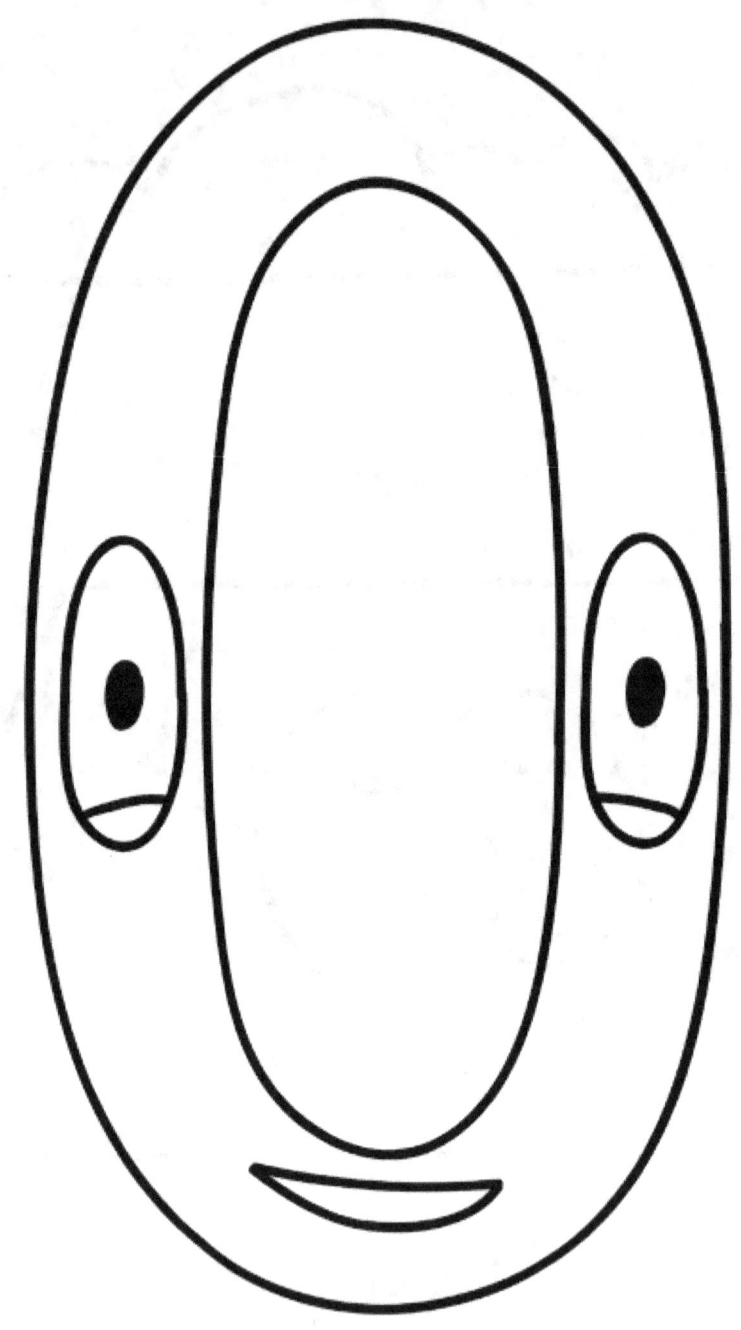

zero

one

two

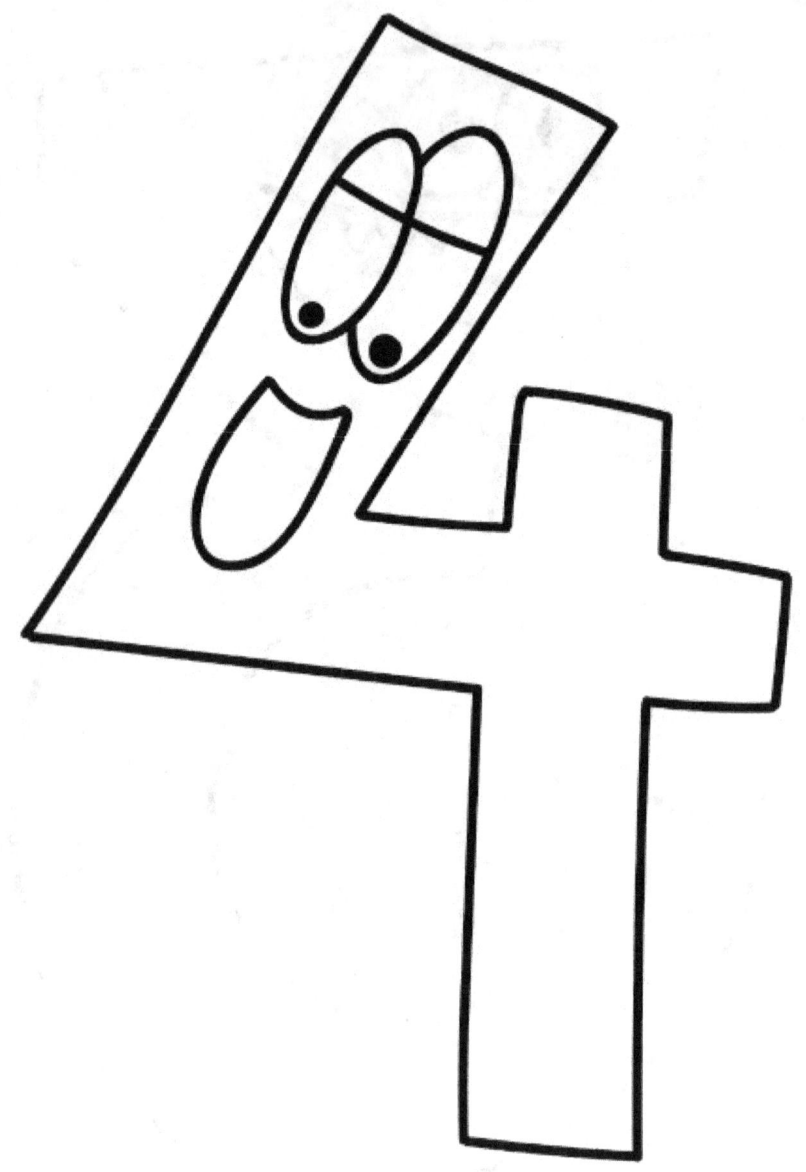

four

five

six

seven

eight

nine

ten

eleven

twelve

thirteen

fourteen

fifteen

sixteen

seventeen

eighteen

nineteen

twenty

thirty

fourty

fifty

sixty

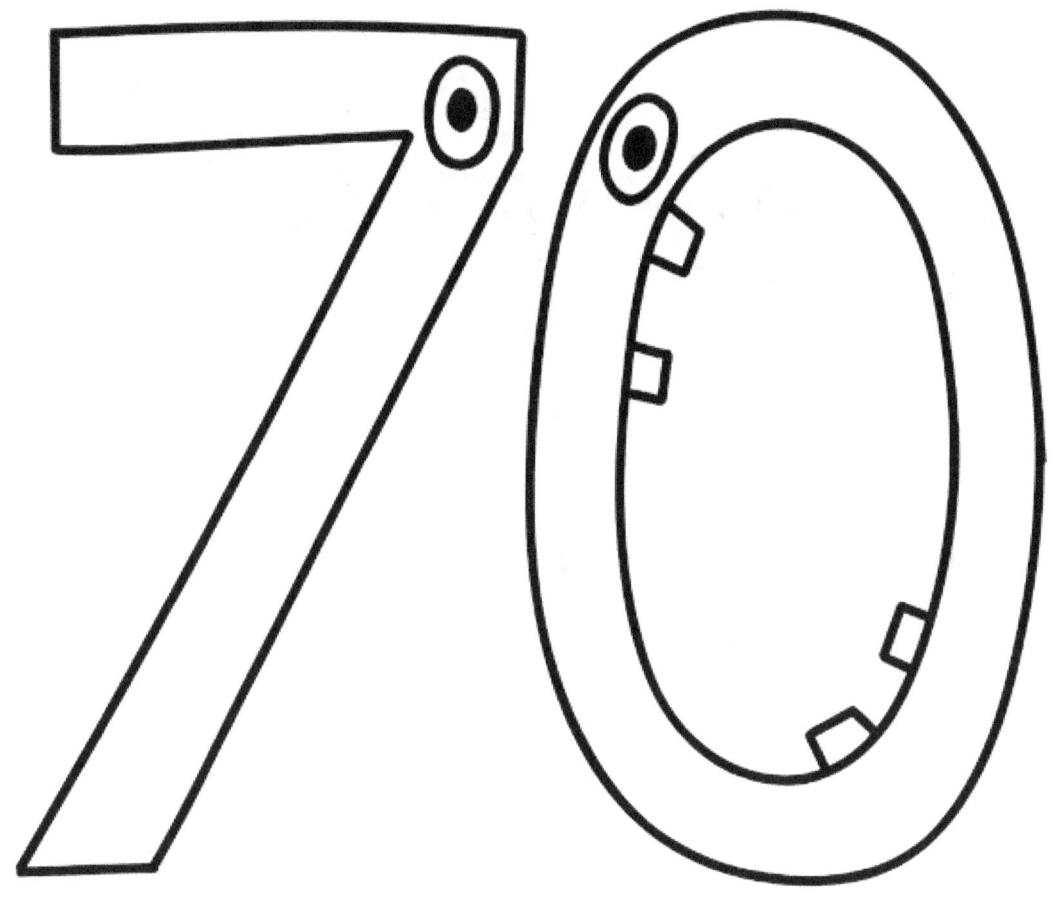

seventy

eighty

ninety

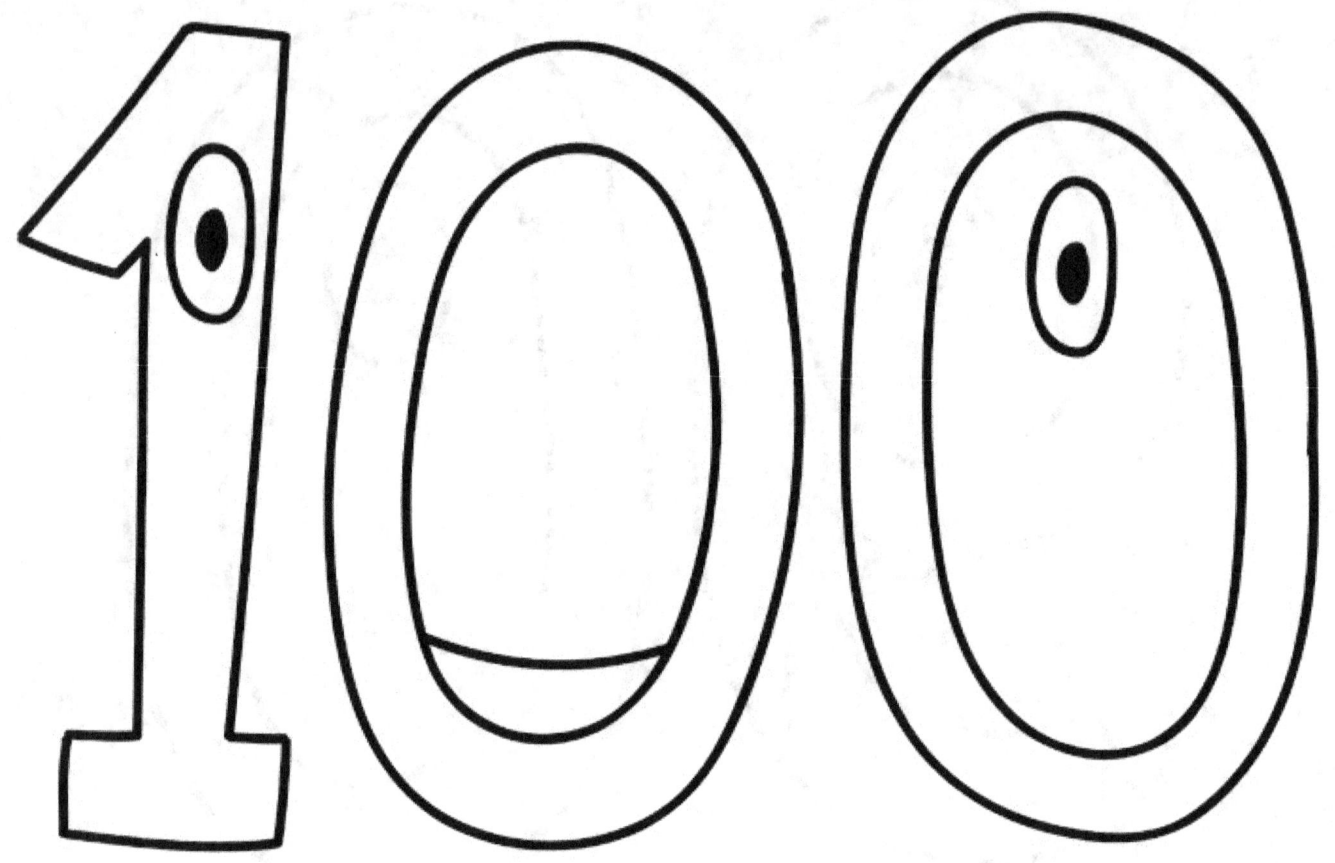

one hundred

Leaves are green

The water and the sky are blue

Snow, ice and polar bears are white

The sun, bananas and lemons are yellow

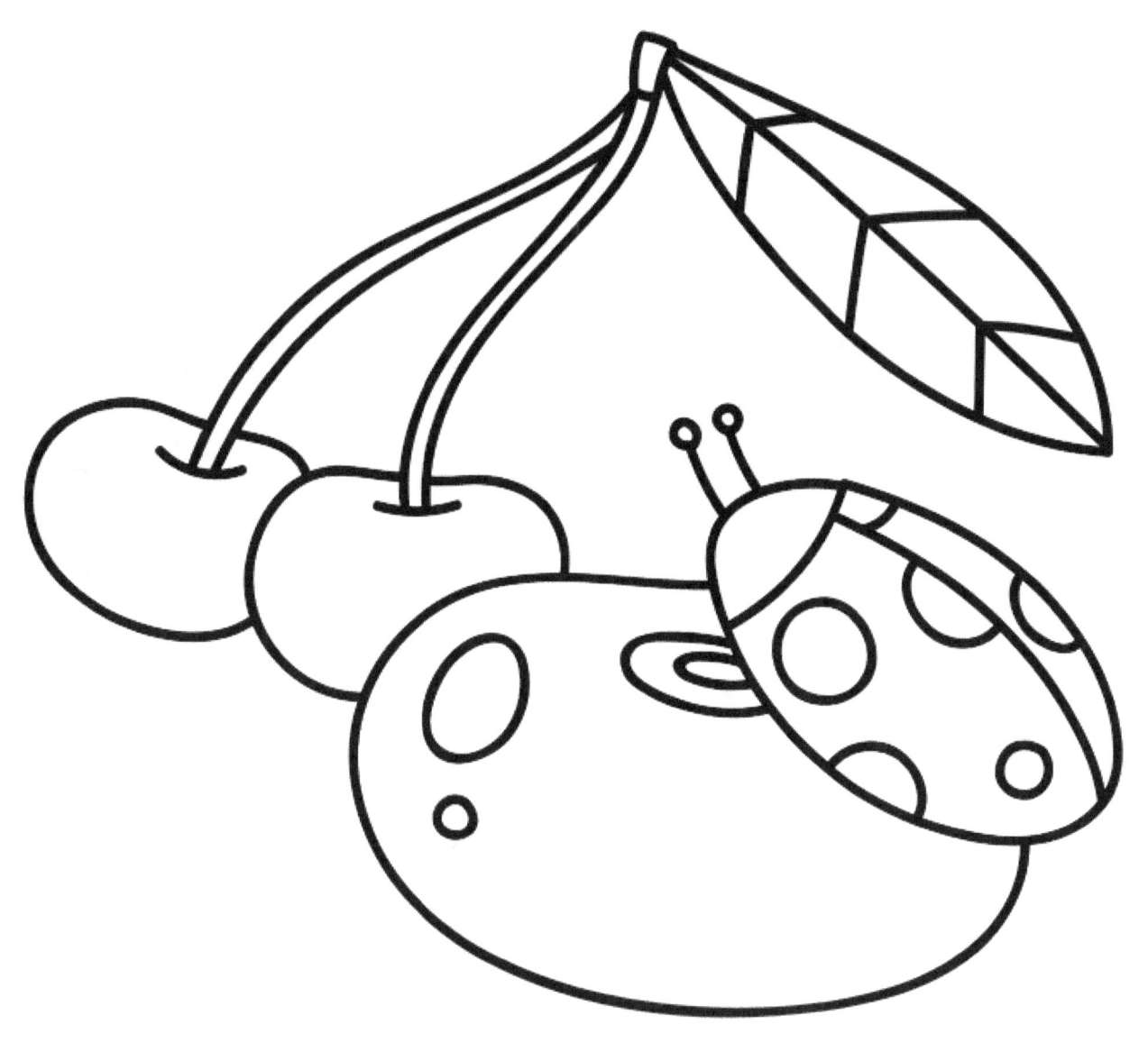

Tomatoes, cherries and ladybugs are red

Pumas, gorillas and crows are black

Peony flowers are pink

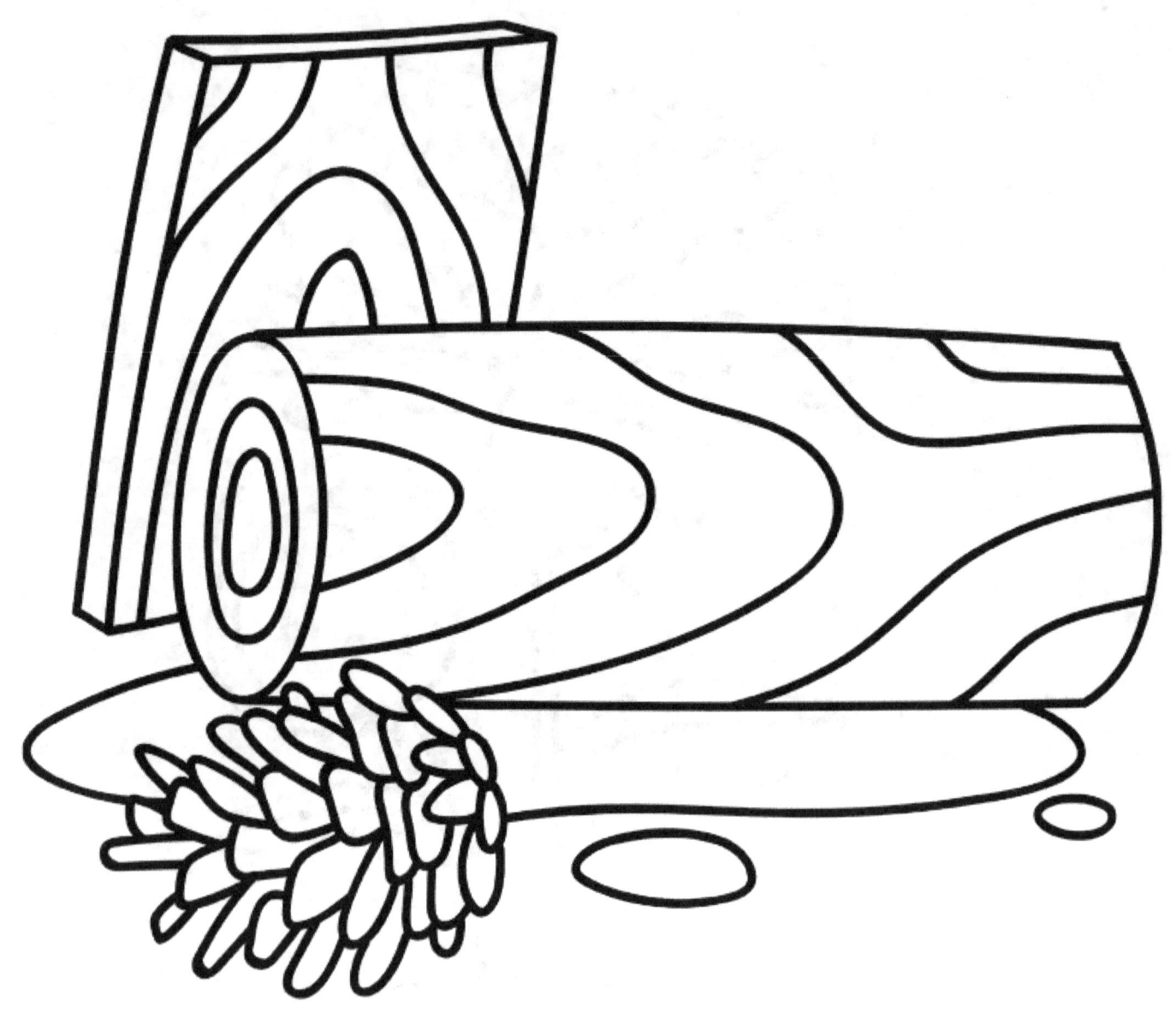

Wood, mud and pine cones are brown

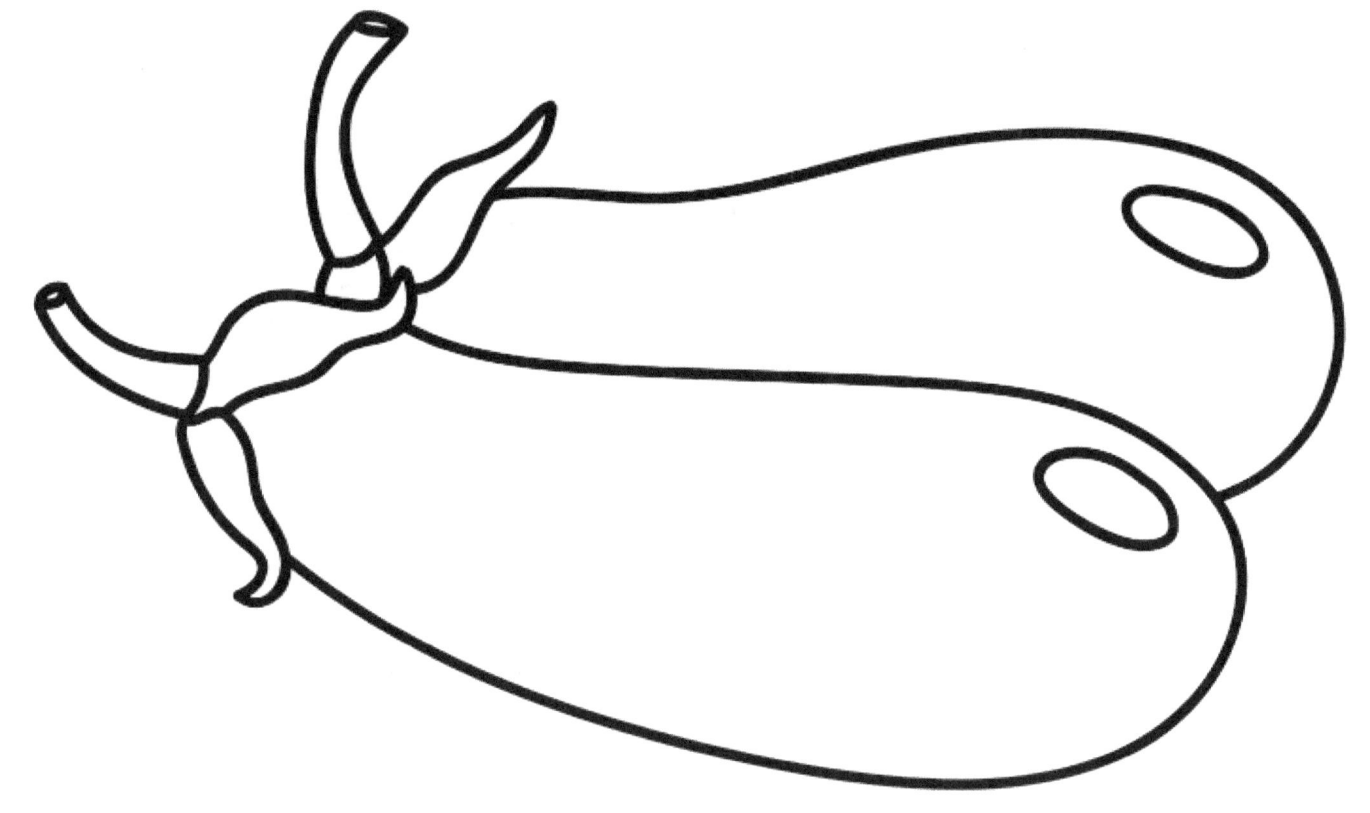

Eggplants are purple

One last thing – we would love to hear your feedback about this book!

If you found this coloring book enjoyable and useful, we would be very grateful if you posted a short review on Amazon! Your support does make a difference and we read every review personally.

If you would like to leave a review, just head on over to this book's Amazon page and click "Write a customer review".

Thank you for your support!

www.ingramcontent.com/pod-product-compliance
Lightning Source LLC
Chambersburg PA
CBHW080022130526
44591CB00036B/2575